I0541785

Dogwood
or
I Would

Dogwood
or
I Would

Louise Salisbury

LitPrime Solutions
East Brunswick Office Evolution
1 Tower Center Boulevard, Ste 1510
East Brunswick, NJ 08816
www.litprime.com
Phone: 1-800-981-9893

© 2024 Louise Salisbury. All rights reserved.

No part of this book may be reproduced, stored in a retrieval system, or transmitted by any means without the written permission of the author.

Published by LitPrime Solutions: 11/01/2024

ISBN: 979-8-88703-432-4(sc)
ISBN: 979-8-88703-433-1(e)

Library of Congress Control Number: 2024920658

Any people depicted in stock imagery provided by iStock are models, and such images are being used for illustrative purposes only.

Certain stock imagery © iStock.

Because of the dynamic nature of the Internet, any web addresses or links contained in this book may have changed since publication and may no longer be valid. The views expressed in this work are solely those of the author and do not necessarily reflect the views of the publisher, and the publisher hereby disclaims any responsibility for them.

Perpetry

This is me a perpetry

Of hands and feet

And thoughts and thighs

Gerbil babies running wild

Dolphin lady in a car

This is me a sitting here

Windy in the summer sun

Waiting for the time to come

To come and run

And roll its reel

And watch and walk

And feel the feel

This is now!

The summer sun

The warbling

And the work undone

The time of day

The time to come

And warmly roll and reel

And shun…

The now is come

And come to be

The dally girl of filigree

The lazy walking down the street.

My Heart's a Ruddy Stone

My heart's a ruddy stone
With time upon it.
I wonder if it knows
Or if it goes
From now till then
As if it were forever
Or as if it were never
Or doesn't it give a damn?
My heart's a ruddy stone
With love upon it
Hate upon it
Fate upon it
"Will you love me now
Or love me not at all?
As the years go by
Will you love me
Not at all?"
Fickle heart! How can you?
Loyal heart, how can you not?
Twenty years and you have
Never missed a beat.

White Spring

White spring

Cover me

Wrap me up

In a shawl of mercy

Comfort me from the tears

Of one who sees

Take me to a place

Where another breathes

White spring

As you see me

Tender me

With the love of living things

And send me

A tender love who brings

White spring

Back to me.

Languorous Lady

Languorous lady
Walk your feet
Sun warmed earth
Smells so sweet
Rooms with kitchens
By the week.
Does anyone know
What day it is?
Can anyone
Its secrets speak?
A day of room
A day to wear
Like summer clothes
To play in.
Languorous lady
Walk your feet
Sun warmed earth
Smells so sweet
Rooms with kitchens
By the week.

Kangaroo Lady

Kangaroo lady

Pouch full of food

Coffee and donutted tummy

Warm like mother's blood

Feel of autumn

Hustle to the brood

Shy Chinaman tractored by

In orange steel papoosed

Watch out weathermen

Kanga baby on the loose

Pouch full of secrets

Happy sigh mood

Pouch full of harvest ready

Time not to lose.

Harmony

Harmony

Two notes blend

Right and left

Pair of hands

Salt and pepper

Woman and man

Harmony

Two notes blend.

The Color Red

My Daddy loved the color red.
He'd say hold up this red shirt
And I'll take your picture.
My Daddy loved the color red.
He'd say doesn't Mommy look pretty
In her red dress?
My Daddy loved the color red.
He'd say get your stinking carcass out here
And carry in this milk.
My Daddy loved the color red.
And I loved my Daddy
With a terrible hurt.

My Daddy worked at the Post Office.
He stamped packages, he stamped me.
He stamped me with his pain
With his guilt
With his milk-cartoned curse.
He stamped me with the color red,
With the ancient ache of third,
He stamped me with his visions,
And he stamped me with his words.

Could There Be?

Could there be love?

Could there be a patient waiting?

And a way of understanding?

Could there be a finder of peace

And a keeper of fragile secrecies?

Could there be a love to come

And a waiting

Patiently?

Dec 20, 1971

Prism

Locked

The jaws of night

Taut

The veins of memory

Chalk dust

The remains in sight

The midwife yields no delivery.

Caught

The bond prisoner of night

Tearing from rope free

To chain…

Be silent cruel recipe

Of a devil blamed life.

Be silent talker ropes,

Be silent talker chains,

Be silent talker…

Fight for an overlooked prism

Of loft curved light.

What in Vacance Comes

What in vacancecomes

Defeats what jades

All others

Wondering where

Insentience crumbles

To bleed with half-formed

Brothers

Rape of method

Ruining pleasure

Come undone wish

Found in heather.

To Be Bride

In this darkness from

What holds me

To this chafe

Of wed entangled burials

Leaden rote

Upon this face?

From this chalice occupied

By what honed

Medieval base

From what parapets

Disguised

Into what arms

Carbon flies?

With Child

When in brink of summer done

Beyond which

We know not

Tethered will be

To a daughter/son

And shaped by odder thoughts.

Globen middle overdone

By mortal thunder wrought

Regale in pain shed

Cord enlocked in wanting

Start and stop.

Fear Invites the Eyes

Fear invites the eyes

To conspiracy

Plain metal disguised

As atrocity

Titans the risk

Of elves perceived

Widens the brain

Narrows the sleeve

Sliding in sane

Perishable me.

Dog Water and Sand Cuffs

Flagrant relish in winds

Voracious voluptuous binge

Relinquish to carousel whims

Cartwheel without permission

Waste matter

Relish mustard

Seize beyond submission

Caste lots with seamen

Elope with darling demons

Flush warden reason

Shake off

Dog water

And sand cuffs.

Begin My People

Begin my people
To make belief
To stable the lost
Won Coventry
To quester the coo
Of pigeonry
To shelter the newborn
Symmetry.

Begin my people
To weld to earth
The coventry lost
Won symmetrical birth
Begin and weld yet
To the earth
Shy fission of mass
Dry celestial thirst.

Dearborn One

Dearborn one
You're gonna be here soon
Your mama is ready
And your papa is too.

Hope you like us
I hope we like you too
Gonna do our best
Our very best for you

Dearborn one
You're gonna be here soon.

Afterbirth

Baby babybaby

I can't believe you

You're blue and red

And your head is a perfect

Perfect shaped egg.

Baby babybaby

I can't believe you

You're blue and red

And I baby, I'm as weak

As a newborn kitten.

What If?

What if when my son is grown

He remembers his mother

Ate her chicken bones

With one breast out

And one breast in

And a trail of soup

Running down her chin?

Oct 2, 1972

Fair Weather Child

Such a one
Who's eyes beheld
A purple worm
Mid whirl of wealth
A two-sided timepiece
Stores to tell
A clay bird dances
Upon hearing a woolen bell.

Winter whistles
Spring whispers
Summer ambles
Autumn golds
Fair weather child watching
Carries arrow and bow.

For Jason

Little one

Just begun

People are so

Weary weary.

A quiet room

Belongs to you

And living soon

Will fill it.

A cross at hand

Beyond it stands

A chariot to Gillian.

Through carnal land

Go forth a man

Led by his pine

Green spirit.

Taken with Notions

It's that ten-year-old feeling

Complete and regular bliss

A Miss taken with notions

Folderol

Devotion

Twist

And should she come up

With solutions

The least of which

Would absolve Confucius,

Would she set off a tiff?

Or resolve

After all,

Who am I to argue

With evolution?

Jack-a-Napes

Porcelain babe

With corn silk mow,

In Jacob's tow

Carrageen Virgo.

Diana inlaid

By Jethro sired,

Midwestern jade

Jack-a-napes

Carved fire.

Kenneth Merwin

Veins of horror

I would rather know

Your red blood

Circular flood

Than haunt

A hapless corridor

Hiding.

With reason

To guide me

A gaunt course

Winding,

For northern pike

Or northern lights

We might,

Sweet foe,

Upriver troll.

As Gravity Reckons

Her brains dashed

Made a lasting impression.

Glenn's graduation

Elegy, procession

Honor high

Before temptation.

A simple fall

As gravity reckons

She from a wall

I from contemplation.

Cathedral Knees

Shoulder my back

Tendril thread

Keep me

Flip side of dead

Crisp under feet

Tinted leaf bower

Mid burning trees

Mid burning towers

Happed my cathedral knees

Happed my fetal hour.

Song to a Son

I dream a summer swoon
In the February month
I Diana once
Am nearing June.
By sea or air
The fishes fly
The swallows dive
Beware beware
The faith so sweet and high
And close the little bird
Who croons his mom-meant lullaby.
Blue his color is
The color of his eyes
The sea, the sky
Teach him not how to fly.
The safety pin pleases him
On his gums bite.
His song blasted
Like the miner's lunch respite
My drunkenness is half my pride
My fear but half a net.
Faith hide,
I the pink prize

In gargled praise his half subsides
My chiding inhibition hums along
Half tenor, half respect sing I
This mortal lover's song.

Your Sister's Come

If I seem a fiend

I am

So long by happenstance

Be damned

Infernal cam

Be man?

Cog on!

Reek of me

Stellar sun

You speak of dreams

I speak of dung

You hold a plaque

I hold a thumb

Ensconced in rote

Enmeshed, embalmed

Weak-kneed be gone

Your sister's come!

In Culvert Time

In culvert time
He owns magic
Who cuts his mind
Who cracks his spine
To suck marrow red
Whose Puck is quiver
Inside his head.
He owns magic
Whose muscle is bled
Whose wine is endurance
And whose kine
May be dead.

The World Is a Window

The world is a window

I peruse it still

Like a six-year-old

Tinsel

Or a dollar bill.

Silver Pearl

Silver pearl

Of dignity twirled

Grate of sand

Flesh circled

Burl of gnash

Thought thorough hurled

Through plate glass past

Wist birthday girl.

What the Hand Holds

If what the hand holds
Disappears
At the curl of fingers
I have jewels in my ears.
If tomorrow wears
A miser's cloak
And this hook ear
Rounds sudden hoax
For these moments spill
From hope to hope
Like steppe stones will
A babble brook joke.

No Man's Lad

He stands ravishing

Inadvertently I ask

Uneasy to be apparent.

I rough him up

With an impatient glance

My commands uncertain pass.

His cheek defying abstinence

Pulls back,

A one-year-old

Is no man's lad.

Forgiveness

Forgiveness
Came knocking
At my door.
I thought her
An old whore
Worn and rubbery
Till some slip
Of witness
Caught my poor.
Forgiveness,
I am knocking
At your door.

Subscription to the Earth

I want to subscribe

To the world,

Say, Life, I will be

Your patron,

I will tilt

Your whirl.

Feed me, sensation

Deem me patriot,

Plural earth.

Purge me, reservations

Heel me, patience,

Old world bird.

Beyond accretion

Tellurian worth,

Fiance succession

Inaugurate mirth.

Promise

If I shall have died

No death defiant

But derelict kin

To Ananias

Halved

Spying on triumph

I shall not

Have regaled thoughtless

Nor menial

Begat monotonous.

Have I against

Nocturnal conscience

Pell-melled

Carousel raucous

Promise, grave eventual,

Softness.

Christmas

The tree

Pink ribboned

And cookie hung

The windows

Garland glistened

Parcels given

Pocket plumbed.

Cribbed wood creches

Boy child yon

My own Joseph's

Ameliorate son.

Take Me in Time

Take me in time

To wind up

On a dime

My solicitous lips

Embarrass

Make me shy

From purpose.

I meant my touch

To bless

Instead I mussed

His curls up,

Curls that have led

Me to believe in

Other worldness.

This world I searched

For my denouement

And not finding it

Under rock or brush

Secure my trust

In hopelessness.

While alone

In his room

He sits silent

Convergent.

You sir, are right

But I am wrong

And know it.

How goes that song

The bird sings

In flight?

How goes that

Train whistle?

Blow it.

Oh for a ride

Oh for a flight

And the washcloth

Tong-offered

By the stewardess

Bride-like.

City Girl

City Girl
I'm a city girl
City girl

Got my red hat
Right off the rack
With the turquoise cherries
I wear it,
No turning back.
I'm a city girl
I got married.

Got my red shoes
To kick off the blues
Got yellow rose petals
On the mantle
Got C. Ritz perfume
To smell like the devil
And a cockpit to zoom
Around Seattle (VW)
I'm a city girl
I got manners.

Got money to spend

Got matters to attend

Got a man and a satellite son

Got a ribbon of red

To wrap around my neck

And a velvet belly

Howling for some.

I'm a city girl

I got aspirations!

Sweet Cider Vanilla

My precious hen
If God was of men
His foot would
Your ankle bend.
If plot could amend
I'd have my novella
Writ and distilled
Of hussy pretense.
Sink me, sigh,
Sofa and pillow,
Of drinking laments
Swill me sweet
Cider vanilla.

Sisters

We were sisters.
We played jacks.
I pushed Carol's bike
Up the hill.
At night
You gave me
Rides on your back.
We were both troubled.
We are still.

We were sisters.
We did not know
Our lack.
For potato chips
We would kill.
For two squares
We had better
Keep track.
I wore pathos.
You wore an
Indian jacket.

Regarding the Half-Tangibles

The immaculate perception won,

Her stomach unrelenting

Covered the question

One:

Regarding the half-tangibles

As they laugh

Behind your back

No hearse

A passed flange of cold.

This girl a beauty

With line of grief

Tipped by a flirting

Wine without sleep.

How hurting deep

I touched her meek

Whether a fool

Or whether a freak

She speaks…

She speaks…

The Fest of Elation

Let the universe benign
The living consist
Of shifting ingredients
A glissando kiss.

When perception is bliss
Unutterable fine,
Furl unfurl
Oh woes divine
Empurple twirl,
Callow confine.

When realization creeps
To meet expectation,
The nourished world bleats
The fest of elation!

At Eight

Shelter the swine divine
Poor poetry,
Knot in the untying odyssey
Cork in the surrogate wine.
Unbind the monument policy
Take plates to heaven
Frisbee at the gates
Eat at eleven
Sink sweetly at eight.

Truce

To all lost sweethearts
Of the world,
I am not angry at girls
Nor at the men who
Made them.
I am not angry
More than the pearl
At the grate of sand's
Commanding.

Evening Alert

Cool quiet evening

Softening thinking

Grow bastards,

Orion hung.

Soon and fleeting

This child's meeting

Touch of reason

Touch of drum

Poor he of weeping

Son, starry sleeping

Whisper of wedlock

Whisper of mum.

For she a keeping

Come plea a bleating

Forestall the padlock

Forestall the thumb.

Residue

Fortuitous remnant

Column,

Would-be Athenian

Who's who solemn

Color me

Sweetheart fallen.

Wrack, an herb

Bath brew,

Walk or run

But never shoot

That fat man's gun!

Pouring over soul

As if to find one,

Never doubted

Until I routed one.

Forget-me-not

Dictionary ruled fun.

How shall I appear

In the clinique

Without the sun?

Madelein, Madelein

Soft dog-eared one,

To a lady like you

I, a student, become.

Work undying

Knighting Victorian

Red wealth a bell,

The Hunchback swung.

Question

How can I describe

Jason's bare almond buns

As he loves to run

All giggling

Through the kitchen

With his huge

New boots on?

Feb 25,1975

Out West Printing

In the olden days

I did not weep

Or say.

I kept watch

Over what

They were dumping.

In the olden days

At Out West Printing

Sometimes they

Threw away

Something.

The World

The world
I loved it once
I love it still.

Hitch

I never thought of my body

As a trailer hitch

To pull my fate with.

I always thought of it

As a gift

I was afraid to wish

And opened it.

Mountains Mine

It's taken me a while to say this
But I was a very happy child.
Feeling the mountains mine,
Racing the bouncing ground,
Strolling the incomparable meadow.

The only thing happier is now,
My golden son,
The wing of fortune carrying him along.
His bumpy run
A cautious abandon.
His drunken smile
The sun.

Skylock

Who down

The hey down

Dandy?

Little girl lay down

Candy.

Roll around day clown

Randy.

Miss your little May cloud

Mandy.

How a purple lilac

Brandy

Pows a heady whiz

He-fancy.

How's your purple why not?

Answer me.

Laughing out the skylock

Pasture we.

Round Robin

Roses fill my pout

Warm fists my symmetrical pockets.

Makeshift wisdom

Wand-in-my-bonnet

Old fashioned sister

Not I a sonnet.

How can I Round Robin?

On it.

Conned not father by son.

Conned not God by father.

Wishbone-broke alluring luck

Offering wind

Offering dust

Offering tomorrow

Limbs to trust.

A nurse's rounds

Both soft and ruffled.

Unkempt the clown

Undone the troubled.

A father absconds

With a daughter muffled.

Lollies on Suffolk summer.

Poppies pong

Pooh sups his supper.

Crepe paper zingers

Beginner humble.

May Day or mingle

Toumanova suffers.

J. Truman Smith

Grandfathers

Don't say much

But grit wisdom

Like licorice

Makes black

Between the teeth.

So large a man

Was he

You would swear

He had compressed

That crutch

Stuck up under

An armpit.

You would swear

That oak

Was worried

Lest it be reduced

To a toothpick

Under the weight

Of that farmer's

No longer now.

Jason

Jason,

Spurious person

Whose Mother gafong

Whose Father kabong

Knows what worse

Can only be better

Along.

Cowboy strong

In quirk and cursing

In hurt and mercy,

Yearn for birthdays

Soft-shirted

Fawn.

This Feeling Called Sad

This feeling called sad

Masquerades as mad.

Captions of bad

Confiscate

The wistful once had.

The scraps of

Plaid ribbons

Tied braids.

Song for a Son

When you no longer
Rumple the covers
In slumber
Like some angel
Run abed...
And I no longer
Stumble over
The urgent relating
Of love that must
And cannot be said...
When your boyish heart
No longer fastens mine,
Climbing in endless
Clasping questions...
And when passes
The ever taken chances
Of glancing
Your poignant practice,
Memorizing your sturdy essence,
And canonizing your global
Effervescence...
I will not regret
Though realizing

How useless and

Woven of hoping

Foolishness,

Every attempt I made

To rob eternity

Of reminiscence.

Unshod

What concerns me

Is the rising cost

Of band-aids

For I have bound

My feet

For great music,

Lest I be construed

Illiterate

Or at best

Inconsiderate.

How I approach

The muse

Pinkly tiptoeing,

Eyes riveted

Upon the spot

Where somehow

Unshod

I danced

My spirit out

For God.

On a Path Called of God

On a path called of God
I trod to lose
That sense of blood
To lift that caftan hood
That clouted sense of good.
On a path of rock
The sun baked hot.
I passed the muttered others
Who neither did call nor cough
But hurried on
Their path of God.
And we but simple utterings
Caught in room to rooms
Of talk
The most surprised
The sounds unbuttering,
The message fluttering
After no answers wondering,
Found
Yet at a loss.

A Colorless Girl

Come back awesome girl

With colorless ease

Doing nothing to please

But feed the world

Unfurling her heartstrings

Like ropes of pearls.

Come back colorless girl

With no ethnic grease

With no family seat

Except in arrears,

With no more courage

Than it took to pedal

Down the street,

All the lonely afternoons

You did not weep

But made a career

Of pedaling down the street.

All the only afternoons

You did not keep

The company of fools

But loved amongst

A constant fury.

And loving as timorous

As deliberate,

So not to ransack the ruins,

Returned a colorless girl

But wondrous,

And with more courage

Than it took to weep,

Continued pedaling,

Down the street.

Dogwood or I Would

Dogwood or I would,

Be assured.

Whether tis nobler to burn

Or die driving,

I heard her religion

Was to die smiling.

Where I, a cobweb urn,

Was filled, lie pilings.

Like the ties those

Surfer boys cull

To do their death defying.

How my knees goad the board

With every swelling twelve-year-old,

Decrying like an arrogant gull

Mother-God-Country and the Sacred Calf

Buying.

How I come up each time

Like a pedaling dog after drowning,

And how the ocean sound

And the fear of rocks

Engrossing both waves and bodies

Thus tossed up

Made me joke with some old buddies

I knew not.

The Shadow Kisses

The world is my lover

The cool breeze

Sweetest of all caresses.

The smell of pine

Surpasses remembrance.

Unpeopled, the shadow

My knees kisses.

Come Utter Syllabled Love

Come utter syllabled love

The kind I cannot

Doubt my way out of.

The kind that pours forth

Like a luminous flood.

The kind that all talk's

In the hunt of.

Come utter syllabled love

The kind that still covets the buff.

The place where the knocker

Still huddles and knocks

Is quiet. Come hovel

Your thoughts.

She Walks Unheard

She who walks unheard

And stalks unannounced

The fever bird

To put at rest

The jabber pitch

Threatening to send her

Into an abyss

Without her portfolio,

Without word from home,

Without an extra pair of socks

With a hole in one-not golf-

And the tops all stretched out

So that one's ankles

Could have sham`ed been

Ankles of elephant's kin.

She who walks unheard

Yet hopes in earnest,

Unassured,

And does not fall

But crawls without witness

And, finally, for the good of all,

Dragging the compressed gases of pretense

And hurling them quick!

Over the wall!

Anticipating ashes…

Everlasting fall…

Afterwards calm.

Hugging the dirt with thanksgiving.

Tenderly calling some rough tree trunk

"Mommy."

She waited for word

But heard a mourning dove's song.

She walks unheard

A tree trunk's fawn.

Marilyn

Unencumbered by my corseted culture

She resembled a shy Highness.

Her caulk white cover encased

Black diamond baguettes

That looked upon the world

As on a favored pet.

Like a skeleton jitterbugging

In Halloween ecstasy

Her passions portrayed

Divine rascals at play.

Her friendly skirts attracted,

God knows who had to be turned away.

For modesty she was gay.

A total stranger

She became as second nature.

A cluster of Medician mendicants

Hovered round her head.

She called herself a tourist.

At her funeral,

No one will be dead.

Sir Desert

Dizzying dazzle Sir Desert,

Are you flowering

To dare me,

To flaunt my folly?

Just because I'm leaving,

To wreak an apology?

"The audacity," you declare.

"Who could want elsewhere?

My ravishing reds,

My apocalyptic pinks,

My preposterous purples,

My whopping whites,

My yelping yellows,

My crimson corals,

My Birds of Paradise

Stopped in flight,

My gargantuan cactus,

My phenomenal, phallic

Palm bananas.

My brilliant, broil of beauty

All but bites the eye!"

Apprehending an answer

I cannot deny, "Sir Desert,

You are diamond like.

Hard and hot and refracting

Pure light.

Uncontestably beautiful,

Sumptuous to the unusual,

And at first,

In your laser beam shades

I delighted to an outrage.

But now my eyes ache

For a subtler sight,

For laundry day blue,

Unbade green,

Forlorn white."

Sunnyside Up

Sunnyside up I landed,

Dropped by a hawk

Who had pegged me

As breakfast.

Our new house,

A nowhere spa,

Designed for a mouse

With brew-ha-ha.

Flapjack flowered

Comme-ci comme-ca

The hillside showered

Carefree-a-la.

What with Wendys

And Jennys that

Hang out windows

To talk,

Small the Wendys and Jennys

Not small

The small talk.

Hurry in Seattle, Upside Down

Hurry in Seattle, upside down

I'm a dash-hound

I'm gonna run right off the paper

I'm gonna run all over town

I'm gonna snoop and stoop

And look all around round round

I'm gonnadootdoot the doot

I'm gonna ooh-la settle down.

Got my raincoat out

Gonna put it on upside down.

Oh I'm sure to get rejected

By the citizenry of town.

I'm not bored enough

To get respected.

Go ahead and beat the brown.

No one claps a frown

On my forehead.

Inside's my accepted

My feather headdress

My feather bedness

My clown.

Dalmatian Morning

At last I have come

To a cool place in the sun

Where every breakfast

Dishes up freedom

Where necessity funs

And Dalmatians pun

On a see-saw lawn

Like black punctuation

Their masters cannot

Read them.

Multitude Boy

Catch me with that contagious sickness
Round out my cheeks, baffle blissness.
Immunize not school children against it,
But kiss them, miss them
Piss on the fogie-goad lessons.
Snatch me a peek
At that Multitude Boy
The one with the no-nap insistence,
The one with the rubber dinosaur collection,
The one with the Mighty Mouse conviction,
The one who supposes glory,
Who knows migration,
The Monarch's story,
The one whom birthdays compel like arenas.
Matadors, take your Disney ears off,
The bulls are having a picnic
On a red checked tablecloth.
The centerpiece is waylaying Christmas.
No one can prevent us
Save those who concoct
A polygamous raspberry sherbet.

Laze

Today I spent
Most superficially.
Usually I leap where
Running is required,
I run when walking
Would get you there,
I walk while others
Sit on their buns
In chairs.
Today I did not talk
If a grunt could convey,
I did not stand
If I could lay,
I did not eat
If I could bathe,
It'll take at least a week
For that hickey to go away.

For Effort a Pyre

To absorb and send desire

To aspire and be quick

About mending.

To coal the fire

And to colt's sire

To be for effort a pyre

To descend crackling, higher.

Widow Queen

Throughout the Baptism

Of wallpaper scraping,

Ceiling sanding,

Floor painting,

Curtain making,

Through each summer window

Come Chelsea christening

Fleur verdancy beckoning

Seduction suggesting

A rainmaker's reckoning,

The widow queen, Seattle

Purrs...

And extending her foot of fur

Sighs highly,

Try me.

And how I will,

And how I would like to.

In the City of Lost Angels

In the city of Lost Angels
The prettiest were crippled.
The crooked old man
With one very short leg,
One very humped back
Which still attempted straight,
One very crumpled hat
To be gentlemanly with.
In one very fumbling hand,
He trusty inched
His stand up camel walk
A far from casual distance,
A block.

And the Messianic spastic girl,
Riveting,
Her twelve-year-old Spanish majesty.
She gave me the peace sign
Because I waved goodbye.
I wanted to give her everything.
Her onlooker mother,
Vendetta vendor,
Glared at our love affair,

Total strangers!
Amid the quiet earthquake
Of her limbs,
It took her three full minutes
To get those two fingers
To stand up right.

Growing Up

How much silencing

The pack of wild dogs

Barking murder and

Make love

It takes to

Grow up.

Dancing

How lovely to share heavens
And traffic earths
By dancing.

How shyly touching
The lifted curtain.

Air

A cool drink of air

Ah yes

I could use this

Cool drink of air

For which I need not sweat

After which I need not compare

Like a deep kiss

This cool drink

Of air.

Third the Leg, First the Face, Then the Hand

Third the leg, first the face,
Then the hand
By command unspoken
I am the talisman.
Banned but not broken
Standing with the under handed
In understanding forming.
A token handy
Like a penny for thoughts,
Direct me to the afterlife
Or to catch a local bus
"Transfer, please."
Mr. Bus Driver,
I wanna get off
At Pearly Place East.
Laugh or sculpture me a necklace
Of this pace. Speed-greedy reckless
Not content to wait.
Not meant to breakfast
Bent not to be late
But carefully inspected,
In costume, relate.
How the Heavyweights protected

From an unsuspecting gait,

Magnificent perplexus,

Gratify an item great,

Small in politic,

Dipped in question,

Galled in Hollywood,

Tall in progress.

Face the word

First the bait,

Then the breath,

Now the havoc absurd

Then come heaven abreast.

Face the world,

Cross the plate,

Bless the neck,

Now the habit unfurled

Then the chalice become bird

Fell to yes.

The Final Act

I have a complaint to make
Against dance.

Why is it always
First the Spartan leg,
Forget the face,
Neglect the tending hand?

Why is it always
First the faint,
Then disdain,
Never the stand?

Why is it always
Worse the fate,
Best the grim,
Last the friend?

Why not let the folderol fluff in?
You think the Masters
Would not understand?
Why not enjoy a fine dine at Tastevin?
You think your senses would disband?

Why not crumble erudite longings
Into canticles camp, gypsies' hymns,
Retorts whimsy, instead of bitter's end?
You think your fantasies
Would be bland?

Why not glorify the great
Tempt the tender
Pluck the strand
And wind it gender to gender
To make a wedding band.
Better to wear it late
Than never.
Better to wear it planned.
Its only justification
To gladden
To have happen.

Otherwise,
Up your nose, pink-hosed,
Up your sweat pants, Modern Dance,
Take to the road your mistletoe,
Your homemade brass,
Your tickle-me-so hats.

Let the mold grow
On your Heavy Act.
Take a slow toke
On happiness…
And stand back.

Pass the pose
And grasp the pass,
Nature alone
Has the final catch.

Gas the gross
And match the flax
Nature alone
Catches the final act.

Not the cigar man
Not the ballerina damned
Not the Avant garde ash
Not the organization cash
Nature alone
Casts the final act.
Nature alone
Calls her orphans back.

Christmas Remisses

I came with surprises

Not with the untold stupendous.

I came to bring awakeness,

To fasten on fortitude,

To peal blasphemy and beatitude,

To wish you a Merry Christmas.

It was my fortune

To be born in darkness.

And out of darkness

I learned fluorescence:

How to take a plastic snowflake

Squeeze into a closet's day-midnight,

Cup my hands around paid-attention,

And just detect the faint lavender memory

Of a snowflake's white existence.

I knew this was not tainted.

I knew there was ever a fight.

There now,

My son wears an Idea bracelet

His property is that of shining light.

Back on Christmas we would wait

To open our presents

Until the sharp words were knifed.

And still I would cherish that word
Rhymes with isthmus.
Later the hospital was brought by Christmas.
Brought by bandages, shots,
And more night with less interest.
This night, of sleepless solitude,
Like the feeling in prisons
Quiet, subdued.
The threshold existence
Of Death-welcomes-you.

But oh, the jelly-middled raspberries
Presented in dishes
That glistened,
The Mrs. Hefley's fudge,
The Mrs. Hill's brittle,
The Divinity without ministry,
Applying the everlasting test
To the glue of your sanity
Tugging-at-war with your senses
Mischief winning.

Extravagance has brought me yawning
To this charismatic gathering.
I am still the fawn

Auditioning for Christmas-mattering.
Elsewhere, reindeer are bombing
On stages disarmingly pretty
Santa, now residing in Panama,
Is putting up tent-striped awnings.

I have told the darkness, Goodnight.
There is no fright left in me.
I have camped nightly
By the light of a snowflake's memory,
With the wool of a
Man-animal beside me
And the torch of a wrong-sung song
Gone rightly.

Folksong for a Nuclear Village

The world in its spin
Arrests in apprehension
When perilous whim suggests
Revenge! Rescind!

Yet the long forgotten enters
On crests of continuance
And amends…

We are given to choose
In generous succession
Every constituent
Every element
Every possibility of pleasure
Every derangement of outcome.

And through the remnants
Of trial and transaction
Extend filament-like
A whispered of
Holy access.

The Assumption of Our Lady of Pockets and Apostrophes

The world
Its timed existence
Asks questions.
Do you see? Echoes Canyon.
Do you hear? Asks Ocean.
Do you remember? Wonders Sky.

A small spinning planet
And its inhabitants
Having arrived once as foreigners
Confess their vulnerability
(As an aside soon to be forgotten)
And become confidants:

A bubble, in orbit,
With propensities to self-destruct.
A spider,
Commanding the delicate spanse
Of a web.
A monkey, whose jump of joy
Masquerades as a toy.
A slinky, whose muse it is
To stretch the truth.

A pair of shoes, made here,
To walk on the moon.
A rubric's cube, colliding confusion
With a conspiracy to learn.
Some seeds, who make
The promise to return.
A nuclear reaction,
Taken by some to be medicine.

To own the world
Became a suggestion
Which everyone heard.
The spider, the shoes tried,
But met with resistance.
The slinky's grasp of the situation
Remained ambiguous.
The monkey persisted
His odd celebration.
The rubric's cube calculated
According to the laws
Of probability.
The bubble made one final outburst.
The nuclear reaction simmered
Waiting for someone
To take his medicine.

The seeds, from within
Their dark surrender,
Ignited.

From "Folksong for a Nuclear Village"

Jason at Ten

That velvet rose
Too red
That fragrance
Too heavy
As the feeling of wine
In my head.

That memory of sweetness
That smile
That son
That childhood sped
Too soon gone.

Before Elektra Came

How we waited
And painted the air
With your attributes.
Difficult virtues,
Nonetheless fair.

You were as yet a yarn
Apart…
Yet always a part.
A tale spun by hearts
Yearning for proof of existence,
A thumbprint, a heel in soft cement.

Fearing a scar in the stars,
Hoping for deliverance,
We waited.
Counting on nothing more
Than your entrance
From Timeless Mind
That thought you into presence.

Miracle Child

Yes, yes my miracle child
You are here and a perfect halo
Of mystery surrounds you.
You lie basketed
In a ribbon wrapped rainbow,
Softly blanketed, desires melting,
Speaking of a silent unbroken heaven.
I, from my broken station,
Adore you intently,
Every passing suggestion of eyelid
To eyebrow,
Every nuance of mouth expressing
The almost.
The little seashell ear
Coiled against the dark silken head.
Beginning with me
And ending with Infinity,
You slowly prepare
For your particular destiny.
And from the close comfort
Of belonging
By dynamite launched, undaunted,
You are decidedly moving on.

Baby Elektra Sleeping

Sultry, sleepy being

Born, a song, amid screaming.

Drifting from evening to evening

Sifting sensations of

Needing,

Feeding,

Screening the void,

Waiting to toy

With the proceedings.

For joy…my love

For joy!

Vocabulary and Visions

My thoughts become
The contours of your face.
Again I take the pell-mell plunge
To the depths of your blue gaze.
Your little fist is closed so tightly
I know nothing will be missed.
Even as you nurse, half sleeping,
You are alert.
Only a fool would say at ease,
There is too much to perceive.
You have staked your claim
Like a Texan on my heartbeat.
Someday I will plead for my release.
Until then, nothing can compete
With your belly button.
Your thumper feet have kicked off
The world's cutest booties.
Your hands steer a wobbly sports car.
Your smile leaves me teased.
Your baby discourse is
Romantic, Italian,
Investigative, Russian,
Comparative, cosmopolitan.

I am invited to intimacy

By the high notes,

Courted confidentially

By the lows,

Informed incidentally

By the middle tones.

(I would say yes to anything!)

Growing impatient, we

Begin to make the rounds…

Dining room to living room,

Hallway to kitchen,

Looking for vocabulary

And visions.

To a Baby Girl from an Old Boot

Trolling for consciousness
You have reeled in my heart,
Snagged it like an old boot,
While I play my part
Of washerwoman,
Companion-in-arms,
Symbolic person.

I go out and buy
Red satin shoes
The size of my thumb.
You look nearer perfection
Than I remember
Ever having come.
I steal a cue
But wonder if after all this
I will be only an impersonator
Of a muse.

You are so cute
I pretend not to mind
The refuse.
My thoughts try to twirl

A knot of concentration,
But are brought back
To the dutiful kitchen.
Refrigerator door in hand
I stand looking
For excuses.
A morsel that was
Once delicious
Ends up in the basin.
I marvel at your salient expression,
Even throw-up looks good on you.

I search for words
Like the last person
Left standing in a train station.
I search for conviction,
For truth,
Or a good enough reason
For all my faults to be
Reduced to a mission.
I no longer appreciate
Even my fortitude,
Although it was the price
Of your admission.

As you are outgrowing
Your basket, so I
Am outgrowing
Being an invalid.
One of these days
I am going to be asked
To shoot:

"Shoot from the hip,"
They will say.

And my aim
Will be that
Of an Old Boot
Improved.

If this were the sixth grade,
It would be a hot Friday.
I would be feeling cool.
I would be in a relay race
Running fast
With a stick in my hand
For you.

A Princess, Piled High

Like a piled high princess
You contentedly sleep
Between two soft continents
Of upholstery.

The bleat and coo
Of your baby news
Echoes in a fond din
Around me.

Your smile causes
Former artists to pause
And say, "Your Highness."

You were munching
On the skirts of your dress
Like a can-can dancer
In retrospect.

No matter how I try
I cannot turn this lullaby
Into that which purrs inside.

Too late to dream,

I do the dishes

Washing each one clean

As riches.

Honey Bunches

A Valentine kiss
For my little Miss
Honey Bunches.

Hungry for lunches
We take a brisk tour
Of the premises.

Discontent at the prospects
We reach for dramaturgy,
Inquests, glorified guests.

All take on a look
Of happiness
At your extended palms.

A grinning princess
Asking for alms,
Secure in her request.

Suddenly finding pockets full,
No one comes up with less
Than charmed.

Closet Me Not

It goes way back-
My history in closets.
In earliest memory
They held a life that was secret,
A probable dump for shoes,
Toys, clothes, no longer used.
Helpless assets these contents.
But the closet itself
Was a fuse.
Igniting fantasy, mystery,
Regret, fertility.
The silent momentum of time
Mocked the present.
In the closet I cried
For sun suits that defied
My toddler size.
Hanging to one side,
I spied the Garden of Eden sun suits
Their happiness implied.
At two I outgrew the red sandals,
But closet bound they reminded,
As did the sturdy brown shoes
Laced firmly up my ankles,

I was headed for a place
I didn't like the looks of,
A place I had every intention
Of avoiding,
A place called grown-up.

In the closet my worst fears
Were confirmed.
A certain sound in my ears
Pronounced the guilty verdict.
The fact that no crime
Was yet in evidence
Was mere inconsequence.
Given time…I would be found out.
Convicted absurdly.
I believed in my guiltwith
A conviction Freud would
Have lauded, but closeted,
I also found …Truth!
The truth of mystery, of singularity,
Of snowflakes that glow
Lavender in the dark.
Standing on top of my father's
Boat like shoes,
Lurking behind scratchy woolen suits,

No one could find me
In Hide-and-Seek.
But his closet reeked
Of starched defeat.
Closed clothes.
"No options," stated the menswear
Flatly.
I was glad to leave.
Mother's closet was more friendly,
Storing Christmas ornaments,
House-wifey dresses, but an
Adjustment had to be made
For the false premises I detected.
The best closet was anonymous,
Holding the magic key to permission,
Garish optimism, a translucent
Lime green plastic globe with
Red marbles in it.
This globe was success itself,
No doubt about it.
I had only to hold it,
Peer into its inner recesses,
And the sounds in my ears
Would be forgotten.
Forgiven?

Never, but for the time being,

Forgotten.

Was this heaven?

I wasn't sure.

But it was better than

The too bright kitchen,

The too dark bedroom,

The too cold living room.

The closet had soul

And within it my perceptions

Keened and grew bold.

I addressed friends

In fake languages,

Imagined peeing

In front of a crowd,

Found power in my ability

To close a door.

For a moment the unfavorable

Consequences ceased.

And I could almost-

Not quite, but almost-

Reach the string which

Pulled on the light switch.

Hoot-Uncommon

Your smile is rakish

As a strumpet's craft.

The glint in your eye

Sharp as flint strikes fire.

I am no match

But pray for hire

To help ameliorate your desires.

Your hopes toppled

Create enough rubble

To choke a host.

I minister and grumble,

You poke like a bloke

From Ireland's woolly coast.

I'm afraid our wars

Will be as bloody and loving

As England and Ireland's.

I shudder for your protection

Is my command.

If only you were mellow

Or I was bland.

Shhhh… my bonny bloke,

Sound not the trumpet to arms,

But toot uncommon bars

Like Tutankhamen's brass,

My Hoot-uncommon

Mellifluous lass.

Elektra Gabrielle

Wide awake. Intense. Alert.

Devastating. Determined.

Sophisticated. Old World.

Charming as hostess.

Charismatic as girl.

A comet unravelling.

A talker for sure.

Balanced and challenging.

Perseverance procured.

Intelligent. Intuitive.

Ahead of my time

And hers.

Never to be forgotten.

Lover needing a curb.

Regally offered

Giver of kisses.

Tincture of ready and

Rascal resistance.

Knowing. Provocative.

Divine. Demure.

Telephoning expositor.

Ceremonial whirl.

Little Girl Legs

The sun falling sideways on us
Ignited the diorama afternoon.
We tossed our last crumb
To an attractive crowd of ducks
That didn't stay long enough
To notice how incredulous I was.
They turned purple heads west.
You lay down on the grass
And looked up laughing
As you encountered upside-downness.
A dog, fanatic with autumn gustiness,
Charged!!!!
And tipped you over
Hit-and-run by eagerness.
Also fallen, I picked you up,
Destiny had toppled me.
Savoring the graft
Of my gaze on you,
The pout of light
Against cloud,
The panache of little girl legs
In shoes-
You run on ahead of me now.

To the Measure of My Love

Elektra,

Definite and passionate

She pronounces the clamor

Of growing up.

I shudder at the speed-up.

Having been my darling infant

But a moment, though precious,

Already she lines the familiar

Circuitous route of intimacy

And decline.

Meeting careful significant distances

With heady relinquishes divine.

She as I, smitten by impractical shoes,

Hot pink scuffs on a tot!

She not as I, wont of incredible woos,

Steadily finding her mark.

She, cupid of mine, Valentine,

Child of ribbon untied,

Captor of my heart,

Knot as I, impart.

Cupid Mona Lise

A vision mysterious,

Your sleep barely breathes

Keeping afloat

Eye caressing symmetry

Composed as Mona Lise,

A cupid in retreat.

The fingers of one hand

Poised mid exclamation,

An alert to softness,

A poem in patience.

The closed lids of Buddha

Grace you.

The fondest of all my dreams

Escape you.

Me and Honey on a Sunny

Me and Honey on a sunny

In the garden leafy lacey

Promised but honest optimists

Chasing, me and Honey on a sunny.

The air fresh and green

Against our faces wake-up clean.

Up and down

Around the morning

She giggles…

The capture inevitable…

Hyperventilates…

For the thrill.

Elektra

Daring, demanding
Subtle, sensual.

Irascible, impelling
Mastering, musical.

Assuredly quizzical,
Unerringly bold.

Playmate physical,
Infinite soul.

Crocus Hope

In your arms the reign of terror

Is transformed by crocus hope.

I fall into my senses

Like one dying

Sinks into flying.

You are so beautiful

It makes my heart halt.

My knees unfasten

My belly winces.

You are so soulful

It makes me want

To be still and listen

To your heart beats

Curling round me like a ribbon.

Coming back from the dead,

I want to wake up,

Buy flowers,

Go to the store,

Go to heaven.

Feb 19, 1986

Divorcee

These circumstances I regret

And, ashamed,

Must explain the impasse

At this convoluted vortex.

The soul alone

Asks the body

To dance.

Without this invitation

The body fasts,

Forgets,

Forfeits a heritage

Of voluptuousness.

There is a saying:

"In the desert

There is no sign

Which says,

Thou shalt not eat stones."

A stone-swallower takes

Some comfort in this.

Within the four walls

Known as home,

I behave.

On the street,

Impeccably pedestrian.

But within the skin

My bones hunt

An exit.

I write less and less,

Hoping to be spared

An echo.

Meanwhile, the daily test

Of sunrise to sunset

Performed consciously,

Cautiously,

Fearing explosion

No less than boredom,

Considerate of those

Still in need of a nest.

I make as good a hen

As any of them.

Clucking conviction,

Adapting to a ruff

Of feathers around my neck,

As if chickens did not

Make me sick.

Friends compliment me

Their fear held in check.

I sympathize with them

Trying to encourage wilderness.

Like SankaiJuku-

Broken on the cement-

No one wants to see,

Yet no one can forget.

Lately I have been mistaken

For someone who would like to

Join us on Wednesdays

For Bible class.

Having retained no sins

Who am I to resist

The suffocation of saintliness?

With only a stiff upper lip

To defend my sagging shoulder chips,

I thank them kindly and decline.

Thirst

The Mother

Bears the curse

Hears the word

Like a flutter bird

Drop from the tongue

The mouth

First open of

Hungry young

Her searched

And finding

A likely scum

To nourish

And be done

Now thirst

Of unlikely sum

Grown averse

To the method

That siphons

The cup.

How helpless

Is the mother.

How helpless

Is the mother's son.

Reminiscence

Dance was a song

Sung to myself

The reminder of flight

To a bird caged

But readying wings

Anyway.

Peach

Elektra
Wants to have a baby now,
A little child
Who will smile back,
Elektra said,
"I will call her Peach."

Sept 8, 1986

Vow

I will not reject my self

Whether others do

Or not.

I will not deny my need

For truth

Or love

Or blessedness.

I believe in the magic

And wholeness of being.

I will not be partial,

Fragment,

Shrapnel.

I will not defer to hatred

However compelling,

However carefully

Articulated and manipulative.

I will not defer

Even to those

Who think themselves

God.

I will smoke hope

Even if

I smoke alone

Even if

I smoke my own bones.

Jun 6, 1987

Utterance

I am naked.

I smoke cigars.

I am the last Indian.

Split, my body

For love.

Split, my heart.

I am a throw

Of cards.

A draw.

To the world

I close my doors.

To my art

The shades are drawn.

I am nothing

But holy,

And wholly apart.

Consolation

My grandmother's favorite cat,

    Boots.

    Dead.

    Run over.

    Flattened.

In October she writes:

    My favorite cat Boots,

    Dead.

    Run over.

    Flattened.

In summer we visit:

    To find my grandmother's favorite cat Boots,

    Dead.

    Run over.

    Flattened.

Three generations offer
To remove Boots.
Three offers are summarily refused.
My grandmother's explanation:
"It's some consolation."

Pact

This is my vow to you,

Discarded soul.

To hold you in esteem

To call you my own.

To accept you

Unruly in nature,

Pitiful in fragmentation,

Awful in power.

To not run

From sticks and stones

That in seeking your destruction

Would destroy all worthy

Of possession.

To stand regardless,

In the knowledge

That you are truth

You are hope

You are one.

Full Moon One

She came with sight within

With her back turned

Jumping off a cliff

Not to be spurned.

She came with arbus

Already earned.

Not willing to start off

Unheard.

She came to teach her mother

To forbear.

Her father flew the coop

At his leisure,

Second to no daughter or son.

So she took root

In the soil of trauma.

Kicked her goat hoof

Against the ceiling

Of love.

To a Husband, Too Late

You took so much

From me

My innocence

My belief

My family.

But you cannot take away

The love I had for you

That I gave freely

Without reservation

Or secrecy.

You cannot take away

The regret I feel that you

Chose to deny the goodness

Within our marriage

Within our home

Within your soul.

You can take many things

When you turn and walk away,

Still laughing,

From the slaughtered bride.

She will not follow.

But you cannot take away

The sanctity of her faith

That even in the pain of her confusion

She loved you,

Took her vows seriously

I do.

I will.

Feb 18, 1989

Learning

Sigh... so I learn.

But I learn about more

Than they teach.

I learn about what they teach

By the way they teach.

And for many of them

 It is the same lesson

Over and over.

The not yet, not here,

Not now lesson.

Yes is not a dirty word.

That I have learned

Aside from lessons.

April 12,1989

Courage

I see the quiet courage
Of a young man

As you go to work,
Go to school,
Go to your father's apartment.

I can think of few words
That would not be
Found lacking,
So I say none.

My heart without a valentine
Is yet
Not without love.

My son remains my son.

Feb 10, 1990

True Confession

I wanted to be a cat
Whose purpose was
To stretch,
To lie in every available
Swatch of sun,
To rub my fervent head
Against the jeaned leg
Of someone.

And to delegate
With proud permission
Who might
And who might not
Feel free to stroke me
And on which sublime
Occasion.

Parents' Love

We speak a different language

Our words sound blunt and foreign

But our eyes tell a most

Familiar story

    Of pride and devotion

    Of grief and gladness

    Of hope and loss

    Of daughter and son.

We speak a different language

But our eyes hold a

Matching truth

    A parent's love

    A child's blessedness.

We are Japanese… American.

                    Aug 16,1993

Easter Sunday

Jewel, being treated badly.

Louise, trying to be brave.

Calli, thin as a straw,

Wanting blankets, more blankets.

Twinkle venturing forth.

Boo, gaining confidence,

Went in Mikey's litter box.

Mikey, fascinated, just watched

As he stepped out,

One black paw after the next.

Louise swimming, as if forever,

In order for Elektra

To be content.

The phone ringing

At eleven P.M.

It was Michael.

Bless him.

Apr 3, 1994

For Jesse and Gail

Before I realized
That theatre could be
Other than sacred
Other than a knock
On the door of the heart,
Before I became alert
To the absence of insurance,
While I accompanied the soul
On its daily walk,
I choreographed
For Jesse and Gail.
At a time when choices
Were made
Not for being the lesser
Among evils
But for having captured
One's full attention,
Having carried one's whole
Personal magnitude
Towards an open space,
Jesse and Gail danced,
And in the dancing
Was praise.

Moccasins

When I see moccasined feet

Treading redolently

On the warm earth

I know Pow Wow days

Have come and I have gone

To a sweet reunion.

Aunts, uncles, cousins

Step forward

Proud and perfect

In their buckskin,

Their beadwork triumphant,

Their patience grim and ancient,

Their trials elsewhere,

Their strengths sung.

But in particular

It is the moccasins

That inform most

Pre-Columbian.

The sole of the foot

Molding itself to earth's

Sculpted surface,

The soft tread,

The quiet girth,
The human foot
As it sets itself down
In succession on dirt.
The beaded trim
Like a benediction
Blessing the one above,
The two below's
Rhythmic petition.
Moccasins stand under those
Whose understanding knows.

How demure the feet of a woman
Pulsing under the long fall of fringe.

How ready the feet of a man
When like a thunderbird
He spins.

Sphinx

Too many times

The gates of her femininity

Have been maligned,

So sits she

Paws folded

Eyes closed

Lips

Inviting no one

Hoping for nothing

Except peace

Within her limbs.

Beyond belief

Her exhaustion,

Remembering the flirtation

Of an innocent

Raw in the retrospective

Of enfoldment

Drained long since

Of love's fervent

Spawn.

Nov 4,1994

Poem for Elektra

Pure radiance
My daughter's face,
Filled with the slap-clap-happiness
Of the song she's teaching me
The motions to.
How beautiful her abandon,
The warmth of emotion
As she carries a tune
Straight to my heart,
Her hands clapping out
A path for her words,
Her eyes sparkling with
High amusement,
Her youth drawing back
Like the folds
Of a red velvet curtain.

Expectancy

This fall while rising
This mindful forgetting
This tasted fasting
This bind of salt
To solution.

This mind of covenant
And conclusion
This promise, not coy
Of union
This voluminous joy
This stand in seclusion.

Cobalt

For she whose cobalt signature
Cures,

We have witnessed how
Under her blue thumb
The ordinary becomes that
Beyond.

We have witnessed how
By tenacity secured
The white depths are
Plumbed.

We have witnessed her habit
Of laughing
At failed transportation,
Exchanging four wheels
For two,
Two for none,
Until by the jet stream
Of her heels alone
She travels on.

We have witnessed how
Life abruptly turns and,
With it, confidence gone,
Until one cobalt heart glistens
And conversation lasts long.

We have witnessed how
She, too, has witnessed
The life of Louise
The death of JoAn.
Safe in her keeping
These two minor tragedies,
Held gently in her hands.

Not in her, have we witnessed
Failure to understand,
Inability to give,
Pride in destitution,
Being met with her chosen responses
Of kindness, mercy, generosity.

Her cobalt slate
By the hand of Athena,
Goddess of life,

Empress of the ocean,

Procurer of small fishes,

Defender of fluid destinies,

Lover of the expanse cerulean,

Is not in ink

But in carpentry written.

Not in grief

But in hope spelled evenly

And with love's precision.

For Jason at WakaiJuku

Many fireflies

Remarking...

But for you

I would not have run

Arms open

Towards the sun.

Capital Gains

First I lost my love.

Then I lost my profession.

Then I lost the benefits of estrogen.

Then I lost faith in good intentions.

Then I lost confidence in all but the concept of justice.

Then I lost the affection of friends and family.

Then I lost hope of eventual understanding.

Then I lost my hair.

Then I lost the ability to speak

Without questioning my throat.

Then I lost the loyalty of some who mattered most.

Then I lost the ability to sleep.

Then I lost recognition of the face mirrored back to me.

Then I lost appreciation for my own predicament.

Then I lost hope for the future.

Then I lost sight of the fact that

It had not always been thus.

       I was once soft.

       I was once, to a fault, loving.

Now that I am about to lose my home,

My family history,

I am full of curiosity.

When all is lost what gains might capital be?

For Jewel

Our conversations are like

Peonies

Opening into voluminous

Delicate orbit

Our words drawing a circle

Around the precious,

The infamous, the kindling

Which ignites the fires

Of our spirit.

Jan 14, 1997

Still Waters

At all times
Thinking of you
Uncomposed.

Your dark calm,
A surface
I want to ruffle.

Descant the choir,
My voice
No longer solo.

Pitched
      So high…
      So low…
Some frequency
Never heard
Before.

Apr 15,1998

Little Nickel

So eager to ruin myself
After being summarily
Forgotten.

I reach for poison,
Strive for numb,
Attain moth-eaten.

But nothing is sharp
Enough to flatten
The memory
Of your favoritism.

You told me once you were
Not good at deception.
That was modesty.

You lie quietly, accompanied
By such fatigue and self-pity,
No one dares be hurt
By your negligence.

Your suffering so original,
So acute, that in comparison
Everyone else's is trivial.

Trivial as my heart
Broken open.
Not worth a glance
Or back page mention
In the Little Nickel Want Ads.

Sand

Here dreaming

Of one who

Brings me

To my knees,

To that sand-sprinkled

Cement I would be

Supplicant.

Purchased by discontent,

I stand on no promises,

A witness without question.

His uttered wishes

To make me insignificant

To make me past tense

I comply with.

Accomplished in the art

Of sublimation,

I stick to business.

Last night's car wreck

Requires immediate attention.

C&S Auto Rebuild will benefit

From a fraternity brother's

Lapse of attention.

Momentarily, he will fall

Out of favor with his Japanese parents.

They will address him formally.

They will call him American.

Accordingly, I will have

No transportation.

Due to whiplash

My headache will either

Diminish or worsen.

As will my longing

For the one

Who walked toward me

In the burning heat,

A dark stripe,

Causing awe to rise

At every dazzling grain

Of displaced sand.

Jul 30, 1998

No Contest

When the car backed into me
My knees were forgiving.
They turned, attempted descent,
Tried to invalidate themselves
As Target.

"It's over," I thought.
The words succinctly given
The clarity with which
A ball dropping earthward
Pronounces gravity.

My legs understood
This contest.
To forfeit
Their only possible response.

The metal steel mass
Given gas…
Momentum, speed, velocity
Vs.
My soft flesh.
No Contest.

My knees gave way to plie.
My vertebrae cracked
In sympathetic whiplash.

But it wasn't enough,
This forced reverence
Of already sorry knees.

The driver put it in PARK.
Got out.
Walked to the back.
Stood looking at
A symmetry of bumpers to knees,
And talked.

In disbelief
My legs listened.

How much does a car weigh?
One ton or two?
My calves can tell you
Exactly.

My ears registered,
"Is there anything I can do?"

My legs waited
To separate in two.
A necessary secession,
I could see that.
My mouth worded,
"Pull forward.
Call 9-1-1."

The question:
Why was there no rushing?
The driver's hand reaching
For the door handle,
Fumbling in haste perhaps,
Understandably clumsy
In an urgency to pull away
From the mistake grotesque?
Why was there no rushing?

The question not asked
Yet answered through
My legs and back,
Leaves a residue.

Since then, I have been
Congratulated for walking.

And it is plain to see
I am among the lucky.

Just last week
A bus driver was shot.
His whole bus fired
Like a bullet
Off the Aurora bridge,
Onto an apartment complex.
The aftermath headlined:
"Eerie Silence Follows Crash."

It is that silence
That speaks most profusely.
For in it, all the stories
Spill out.

Of Two Children

My daughter is gone

Over a chair

She has left behind

A favorite sweatshirt

One from my son's

University.

I go to sleep

Holding it

My arms containing

All that I love

Therein, of

Two children.

I Am Your Sister

If there is anyone here
Who has known fear,
I am your sister.
If there is anyone here
Who has known pain,
I am your familiar.
If there is anyone here
Who has known hesitation,
I am your defender.
If there is anyone here
Who has loved beyond comfort,
I am your shoulder.
If there is anyone here
Who has lost hope,
Catch the flicker.
If there is anyone here
Who has loved a daughter,
Known her worth to be immeasurable,
If there is any God here
To whom thanks may be offered,
I am your girl.

Tokyo Millennium

Against a red alley
The bicycle blue.
The children precious.
The urban chic boom.
The architecture elaborate.
The cuneiform fumes.
Buddha wrapped
In a red apron.
The incredible food.
Paper knotted onto prayer strings.
The monk whose nose
Required a sleeve.
The palette of timelessness.
The crimp of knees and feet.

Thinking back on baseball,
Old McDonald Wada Farm,
Hula dances, hot springs,
Hello Kitty returns to the U.S.
Well-fed and carsick.
She leaves, loving the city
Where in ironic passion
The worship of the West

The sanctity of the East
Lay entwined like
Millennium's children.

A Mother's Love

Lovely one with the ring

In her nose.

She charms me

With her poetry, her photography

So well-wrought.

She is as beautiful

In maturity

As she was

In adorable infancy.

I shall never

Get over her smile,

Her twinkling eyes,

Her tiny hands.

On her laughter

My heart expands.

All my love

Is unfurled

On hearing her songs.

My number is dialed

Whoever she calls.

My hair falls down

When she shakes her head.

Because of this

I am at her mercy.

Take pity, for

A mother's love

Is willing servility.

Talisman

Light through trees

N D E's*

Mother elephant and baby

Left behind her pink skin

An angel's

Dream of freedom

A homegirl's

Transformation

No comparison

    To wit

    To love

    To life

    Transitions

*N D E's- Near Death Experiences

Oct 16, 2000

For Elektra on Christmas

On this our last Christmas together,
I offer you some small trinkets
To convey all that cannot
Be bought.
My mother's traditions
I pass on to you,
The sewing of a stocking,
The special recipes,
The background presence
Waiting special delivery.

Your gifts to me
Precious and unrepeatable.
A lifetime of friends
Precocious and innocent
Filled my house with youth.
    Ashni, Calli, Wen,
    Melanie, Jeremy, Wesley,
    Michael,
Starred in living room and
Kitchen dramas.

You who have been the center
Of my industry are on the move.
Soon you will recreate
The romance of life anew.
With your unique voice you will
Pen words of truth,
You will find the meaning
Behind many absences,
And you will fight for what
You do not want to lose.
For this boxing may come in handy.

As for me dancing was my Muse.
I hoped to make a common life
Beautiful.
Although no one was fooled,
It was the attempt
That carried
Whatever nobility I possessed,
In truth.
I danced from the soul,
Gratefully.

Dec 24, 2000

Evaporation

Brave it is

To write a letter

Condensed from

The corrosion of years

Into a fine mist

Of words

Thin enough to be

A spritzer.

Thin enough to be

Heard

Without taking pause

Or donning armor

Thin enough to cast

But a shadow

In the path of

The blinding sun

Of indifference.

Walking

She comes in sorrow
Her warm heart
Faltering
After parting first love.

First... Last...
Love is all the same
A master not to be slighted,
Ominous in its ability
To render us woe begotten.

Once a bright flame
Her hopes become
A damp smokescreen.
Her noble intention
Not to be kindling
On the burning pyre
Of loyalty.

From this dislocation
I would spare her
But not from the love
Always sacred, sweet.

She has tuned in
A new song,
"These boots are made
For walkin…"
We laugh.
There is walking to be done
And she has many songs to sing.

Complete,
In quiet harmony
She creates a seashell box
Centered with a compass
To direct her
Where she wants to be.

Do You Remember?

Do you remember
The beautiful child you were,
The huggable one,
The wonderful girl?

Do you remember
Roller skating in a circle
Through the dining room,
Living room, kitchen?
Do you remember playing
With Michiko and Shinya?

Do you remember
Singing in the backyard,
Sitting in the grass,
The lyrics: "Honey loves the flowers,
Honey loves the trees…"
You were Honey.

Do you remember
Getting ready for the prom,
Getting your hair done,
Looking magnificent?

Your youth glowing
 Your heart on a
Rocketship?

It hasn't happened yet.
I already miss it.

May 13, 2001

Literacy

Possible to see
A human connection
In the curriculum of detention.

Shall we read?
Shall we compare word liturgies?
Shall we eat, live, and breathe
Literacy?

For oppositional identities,
The round vowel answer.
Inequality is not inadequacy.
Opportunity is not acceptance.
Goals are not always given.

For some, to kick the ball
Requires patience, concentration.
For some, to center one's hate
In the middle of a spinning sphere.
For some, ignoring the game
Is powerful aim.

Who would tell a child
"Doin steps" is why
We don't think
You're intelligent.

I will ask the sulking black girl
The Athabaskan
The Hopi children
To cure my innumerable illiteracies.

Departure

On the eve of my son's departure

For Shanghai

I hold his future lightly

Resting as a butterfly

On the palm of my hand

Which fans its wings

Until rising

Like paper hands clapping

Faltering...

        Rising...

                Flying...

Upwards he leaves tomorrow

His homeland of Japan

Where he has been accepted

In the warm embrace

Of your family. Of you

He speaks with praise.

My shoulders round

With gratitude.

My prayers search for

Syllables to speak...

        Arigato...

                Arigato...

What Mavva Said

You carry the flag

Of the family.

It is not usual

For the woman.

It is not easy

To carry the flag.

It is something

In your character.

Something gentle.

Something hard.

It is opposite.

It is an inspiration to me.

Aug 8, 2001

Ode to Lukachukai

Since coming to Rock Point and Lukachukai
I have entered a magic world.
It is a world I understand but a little.
Through ignorance I have committed many offenses.
Your tolerance is greatly appreciated.
Though confused, for the first time in many years
I feel truly thankful.
One day, before I went to the hospital,
The sun reached down to warm my frozen heart.
The Yei bi chei were dancing there.
I saw the Katsina in the sun.
Blackbirds and crows guided me
Where I was supposed to go.
The elders humored me
And picked me up when I was lost.
The children delighted me.
Moody gave me a coat with pockets
So I wouldn't lose my keys.
Ben told me about the mist I would see.
The horses walked by reminding me
Of all that on earth is holy.
From the day I learned your names
A fullness has come.

A picture takes shape with the growing power definition.

I begin to recognize who you are.

I see your work.

I see your connection to your students.

I see your bonds of

Community

History

Ceremony

Athletics.

This is the place that for so long compelled me.

This is the place I begin to call home.

Learning takes place without our knowing

Without curriculums

Without a studious habit.

Learning takes place in the Fire Dance

I got lost on the way to.

In the absence of love

In the falling of the stars overhead.

Learning takes place in an old woman's house

Among cradleboards and grandkids and knitted dresses.

Learning takes place bead by bead

Stitch by stitch.

Learning takes place in the shifting face

Of the cliffs

In being slammed down onto the ground by wind.

In the sticking out ribs of the dog

At the Trading Post.

This is the place I want to be a student of

To follow the ways of the clouds

Sage and pinion

To see a sand painting

To witness the ancient steps

To weave a cloth of secrets

To sit unattended in harmony

Hozho`.

If you have learned anything from me

God bless you

For everything I have learned from you.

Not wanting to let go

I wish you

The sun's rays on your cheek

The soft earth beneath your feet

A diehard battery in your pickup

A load of juniper for your stove

And a Merry Christmas full of love.

Remember me.

Dec 9,2001

On Leaving Nazlini

Next week I will be wanted.

Next week someone

Will speak to me.

Next week I will greet

A roomful of hellos.

Someone will linger

To chat with me.

The conversation will be

Rich and hearty

Thoughtful and perceptive.

Next week I will not

Sleep on the floor

With the smoke alarm

Chirping its empty litany.

Next week I will have

Somewhere to go

Some place close

Walking distance.

I will not drive to the moon

Or what seems like it.

I will have a friendly toast

To myself. I will not

Laugh at my need

To hear my name

Louise.

I will hear the phone ring.

I will be asked to go

Some place interesting.

I will return home to a letter

Recommending me for every job

I've applied for.

They will ask me to start

Immediately

For more money than I need

And medical insurance to boot.

I will think about it and

Decide which job suits me best

Which will allow for my

Idiosyncrasies

Such as a taste for humor,

Kindness, and

A sense of belonging,

Fresh air on my face and

A smile crossing my cheeks.

Appointments will be made

That others will keep.

I will not be left with

Nothing to do,

Nowhere to sit,

And nowhere to put my eyes,

Or feet.

My tires will never be flat.

My shoulder will never be weak.

My hair will hang down my back.

My horses will gallop in the wind.

Freely they will come to me

Freely they will softly nuzzle me

Freely I will give them candy

Freely I will leave Nazlini.

Dec 18,2001

Sunflower Daughter

As open as your heart
As bright as the light in your smile
As high as rapture
As wide as tomorrow

Everywhere I see one
Yellow petals surrounding spirals,
I think of your happiness,
My sunflower daughter.

Elk

As velvet

As the morning,

Three chandeliers

Sidestepping dew

My heart stops

In beauty.

July 3, 2002

Akira's Heaven

This fragrant bit
Of Akira's heaven
Reminds me of home.
The black red rose,
The curling sweet peas,
The blushing old fashioned blooms,
The white puff of petals
Surrounding a green eye,
Exude the delicate fragrance
Of days gone by,
When I belonged to the rose,
And the rose belonged to I.

Colorado Springs

Sixth grade picnic
Following suit
Under the Kissing Camels.
The Garden of the Gods
Home to my heart.

Embraced by Pikes Peak
Where my second grade first friend said
Her uncle cut off little girls' heads
And threw them off the top.
She knew because she saw them
On Sundays while skiing
With ants crawling all over their necks.

Pikes Peak was how I knew
The four directions.
Always oriented.
Always secure in knowing
Where West was
Where North was

Where East was

Where South was

Where I was.

Manitou, giver of tourist trinkets

And mineral water

Decades before Perrier.

We would take our jugs

And fill them up

At the colossal statue

Of the Indian man

Stooping low

Pouring out a constant flow

Of free mineral water.

Good for health.

Good for making root beer

To take on picnics

To the Garden of the Gods

Or to the Rocky Mountains.

Colorado Springs

Crystalline snow under

Cerulean skies

Colorado mountains

How I knew God.

Colorado electrical storms

Warned me what's coming.

By Louise Salisbury

True North

True North.

A son who was

The sun to me.

Golden boy

Crowned with the love

Of Large Intensity

And Medium Intensity.

Newspaper mogul

In Junior High.

Japanese Gaijin son

In High School.

Undaunted he went alone

To Tokyo

Searching for his

True North.

Now a man,

A father,

A rock.

At the helm

Of his destiny

He leads those

Who love him

To True North.

June 8, 2024

Writing

I tried to capture it

With words

The fall through time.

I wanted to make a net

To break the impact

Like Cirque de Soleil

An acrobat spinning

By air upheld wielding an image

Of light on the water,

Of ducks walking on ice,

Waiting for the return

Of the lake to swim

And dive in.

I tried to create a box

To put the ether in

Holding it not tightly.

But lightly

As one holds a bird

In the hand, heart beating,

Promising flight among friends,

Travelling south by instinct led,

Arriving rested in the land

Of circumspection.   Dec 19, 2016

www.ingramcontent.com/pod-product-compliance
Lightning Source LLC
Chambersburg PA
CBHW020409150626
46554CB00012B/423